It's a *funny* old World!

Martin Kendall

a BIG thank you for the images used.

Wilson Vitorino
David Clode
Sharon McCutcheon

This book is a work of Non fiction. All of the names, characters and incidents that bear any resemblance to actual people or events are too bad. These events really happened!

©TheDawnMedia

Thedawnmedia.co.uk

Published by TDM Publishing
Paperback ISBN:978-0-9957432-7-4
eBook ASIN:B08S9RMWQD

Dedication

This book is dedicated to my wife, children, family and friends, living and past. In addition to any characters alluded to in the stories who may not fall within the aforementioned categories.

CONTENTS

It's a funny old World!

Preface 1

Chapter 1 3

Chapter 2 5

Chapter 3 8

Chapter 4 11

Chapter 5 15

Chapter 6 18

Chapter 7 20

Chapter 8 22

Chapter 9 24

Chapter 10 27

Chapter 11 29

Chapter 12 33

Chapter 13 36

Chapter 14 38

Chapter 15 41

Chapter 16 45

Chapter 17 48

Chapter 18 50

Chapter 19 53

Chapter 20	56
Chapter 21	59
Chapter 22	62
Chapter 23	65
Chapter 24	67
Chapter 25	70
Chapter 26	74
Chapter 27	76
Chapter 28	78
Chapter 29	80
Chapter 30	83
Chapter 31	85

Preface

I hope that you will enjoy the tales in this book.

The whole project kicked off because I have been amazed at the wonderful cultural differences and experiences the World has to offer, in addition to the absurdity of actions looked at in retrospect. As such I would like to point out that, as the title of this piece says …

'it's a funny old World.'

Might I respectfully suggest that the reader lingers over every word and savours the scenario.

Apologies and explanations are at the end of the book, let's begin …

It's a funny old World!

CHAPTER 1

The man with no name

Many people will meet a well-known person at least once in their lives. Usually the meeting is arranged, an appointment, a function etc. and does not come as a surprise. Imagine, however, the unexpected …

A business associate of mine was having dinner at an exclusive Swiss restaurant a few years ago with his distributor.

Towards the end of their meal three men entered the restaurant and sat at an adjacent table within my friend's vision. As usual in a situation such as this my friend was engrossed in conversation with his associate but occasionally glanced around the room. One of these visual forays resulted in his gaze settling on one of the three men at the next table, noticeable because he was a little shorter than his companions. At the same time his gaze lingered a little as the face was vaguely familiar.

My friend remarked to his dining companion that he felt he knew one of the diners at the table; his companion took a glance but was unable to assist in identifying the individual concerned.

By the time his coffee was served my friend was becoming obsessed with the identity of this mystery diner to whom he could put no name. After their coffee my friend's companion visited the WC and my friend took the opportunity to approach the unidentified man, not wishing to cause offence by apparently ignoring him should they have been acquaintances.

The conversation is reported to have been as follows:

My Friend (MF): 'Good evening'

Mystery Man (MM): 'Good evening'

MF: 'I'm sorry to bother you but your face is familiar, have we met before?'

MM: 'I don't know, but I'm sorry I don't remember you'

MF: 'Perhaps we've met in the course of business?'

MM: 'Perhaps, what business are you in?'

MF: 'Ophthalmology, medical'

MM: 'Sorry, never had anything to do with the medical side of things'

MF: 'Well, perhaps we've met socially, have you ever visited Windsor, where I live?'

MM: 'I don't think so. I've been to London a few times'

The conversation followed these lines for a few brief minutes, my friend ascertaining that they had little in common and the mystery man's companions becoming increasingly amused by the questions and answers. The final statements were:

MF: 'Well, I am terribly sorry to have disturbed you, your face is so familiar, my name is John' (surname omitted for reasons of security, my own!)

MM: 'That's OK, please to meet you John, my name's Clint …

… Clint Eastwood'

CHAPTER 2

Give me the Money

Accountants are a fickle lot ..! They treat company money as if it were their own.

They count the money coming in from sales but absolutely hate to part with it for legitimate expenses. They want receipts for everything. However, it is not possible to obtain receipts for some forms of expenses incurred whilst on company business.

The American dollar must be the most frustrating currency in the World. All of the notes, regardless of denomination, appear exactly the same size and colour. Why the Americans cannot change to a more colourful currency, such as the Australian dollar (not only one of the most attractive but also waterproof!) is beyond me.

There are so many tales of transatlantic visitors giving the wrong note, always of a higher value, that they do not warrant repetition. Suffice to say that the Company Accountant will not accept (non-receipted) tips to taxi drivers of US $100 or more!

Having said that, the US dollar is the most negotiable currency in the World and is always handy in some of the more obscure destinations.

My favourite recollection on the subject is from 1986 when I was travelling the east coast of Africa. To obtain foreign currency many of the airports would demand a departure tax, not prepaid on the ticket but at the airport, in person, in cash, on departure in sterling or dollars.

I had arrived in this capital city a few days earlier and changed £50 in traveller's cheques to the local currency. During the course of my stay I hadn't spent much of this, as the locals were only interested in foreign currency, of which I had little. The hotel bill was settled by credit card in US dollars. In other words, the local currency I had was virtually worthless.

* * *

On arrival at the airport, prior to checking in, I was directed to a small hole in a wall where I was instructed that I had to pay departure tax of £6 or $10. I didn't have this in cash and my credit card was not acceptable. If I were to be a suspicious person, I would suggest that this was due to cash being easier to pilfer. As I am not, I would ask the reader to disregard that remark.

Another traveller's cheque was produced, and I changed up another £50 into US $ to pay the tax receiving the change in US $, everyone happy.

After Immigration and security, I approached another checkpoint where I had to declare all currency on my person. On receiving my declaration, the uniformed officer took me into a cubicle and informed me that, as I hadn't declared the dollars or local currency on entering the country, I could not take it out. I started to explain that I couldn't have declared the cash as I wasn't in possession of it when I entered, the officer looked bored.

Standing in a small cubicle, with a small table between us. On the table were two piles of money. One £50 worth of local currency, the other £44 worth of US dollars. It appeared that stalemate had been reached.

Looking him in the eye I pushed the pile of local currency in his direction, slowly returning the hand to my side after having carefully picked up the dollars. I turned away, removed my wallet from my pocket and inserted the dollars into the wallet. I inserted the wallet back into my pocket.

Returning my gaze to the table I saw that the table was bare. The officer very kindly escorted me out of the booth, pointed the way to the departure gate and wished me a pleasant flight.

CHAPTER 3

Listen to the Experts

'CJD can never be caught from infected cattle'

'Covid-19 is nothing more than a bad cold'

Just a couple of examples of ignoramuses demonstrating ignorance and incompetence whilst hiding under the guise of experts.

It also goes to prove that anyone can get it wrong.

We were attending an exhibition in Jerusalem, more on this later. Within our group was an individual who had visited the city many times before.

When the congress had finished three of us, including the one who had spent a great deal of time in Israel (the 'Expert'), found ourselves with half a day of leisure time. Being where we were, and all of us having the same inclination, we decided to explore the ancient part of the city.

The 'Expert' had already guided us through a number of difficult and unknown situations insofar as negotiating the unfamiliar local customs and so as we approached the gates leading to the old city we nodded obediently when he advised us not to speak or make eye contact with any of the multitude of shopkeepers less we waste the little time we had in extracting ourselves from unsolicited sales 'pitches'.

We wandered through the very narrow, cobbled streets. Marvelling at the sights and studiously ignoring the innovative approaches such as; 'Hello'; 'English?'; 'American'; 'very cheap' and the best one, 'Please come into my shop, I just want to rip you off'.

Three people, walking abreast, filled the narrow, ancient Jerusalem streets. Therefore, the two 'riding point' received most of this incessant barrage. Our experienced colleague, by far the tallest of us I might add, walking regally and untroubled in the middle.

* * *

One aged shopkeeper was sitting, just outside his premises, leaning backwards on a stool enjoying the afternoon autumn sun. As we approached, he said nothing, which alone was noteworthy, he just held out his right hand in a 'shake' gesture.

As we were unable to pass by abreast and as the shopkeeper was on my side I slowed down so as to walk behind our taller, more knowledgeable colleague, who did no more than to offer his right hand to the shopkeeper. In a move belying his age and build the old man appeared to flick his wrist. The proffered hand, together with the body attached to it, was propelled from the centre of the street, in front of me and into the shop with the words 'come see my wares'!

My other colleague and I continued on our way. After all, we didn't want to waste OUR precious time extracting ourselves from sales 'pitches'.

I wonder where John is?...

CHAPTER 4

London Bridge is falling down

Since that day in September 2001 security has noticeably improved in airports and on airlines throughout the World. No longer can one carry sharp, pointed metallic objects onto an aeroplane. However, there are still some anomalies. Why, for instance are small scissors and nail files banned when one can purchase a Swiss Army Knife from the on-board shopping catalogue on some airlines? I would prefer to face an assailant bearing a nail file than a shattered one litre glass bottle purchased from the duty-free shop. Airport restaurants provide metal forks, yet plastic knives. Some airlines provide their Business Class passengers with metal knives, one can only assume that hijackers would not go to the expense of a Business Class ticket!

In certain parts of Asia cigarette lighters and matches are not permitted through airport security although at a stopover en route one can usually purchase a lighter to satiate one's cravings.

I am afraid that these anomalies do not serve to persuade me that my personal security is any the better. However, let me relate a particular story....

A good number of years before '9/11' I was travelling to America, San Francisco, for an exhibition. My employers at that time had a sales office in Atlanta, where the year before the Olympic Games had been held. One of my colleagues had been working from the US office at that time and had purchased for his father-in-law a paving brick which formed part of the Olympic Way. These bricks were a commercial success and the sponsors' nominated name was permanently engraved on the brick with an identical copy being retained as a momento.

Unfortunately, the copy was not ready in time for my colleague's return. When he knew I would be travelling there he asked if I would collect the brick from one of my US colleagues who would be attending the exhibition and bring it back for him, I readily agreed as I did not envisage this causing a problem..

I duly took the article from my colleague, it was packed in a very sturdy cardboard box, with polystyrene packing protecting what I can only describe as a paving stone, some 9 inches by 4 by 3. (For those not accustomed to imperial measurements, multiply by 2.5 for an approximate metric equivalent.)

Seeing as the item probably had a certain amount of sentimental value, I decided to carry it with me in my briefcase rather than send it back in my hold luggage at the mercy of all and sundry. This seemed like a good idea at the time…

I arrived at San Francisco International Airport some 2-3 hours before the flight. The last time I had departed from this airport was a few months previously and smoking was permitted in certain areas of the departure lounge. Please don't judge me on this, I've already had the lectures!

In the meantime, the authorities, in their wisdom, had decided that passengers travelling from the airport, particularly on intercontinental travel, would not want a smoke. (At this time smoking was still permitted by certain airlines on board but most certainly not on any serving the United States.) Therefore, the only place to have a cigarette before I landed back at London Heathrow was outside of the airport terminal where the taxis were.

Being blissfully unaware of this I checked in, proceeded to security, placed my briefcase on the conveyor belt, my keys, coins, mobile phone etc. in a tray and walked through the metal detector. On the other side the security guard was holding my briefcase and asked me to open it. The open case revealed a cardboard box, which I was instructed to open. The Olympic Paving Brick in all its' glory beamed at us.

Now sometimes one says the first thing that comes to mind.

'What's this sir?'

'A brick.'

* * *

The security guard looked at me with a blank expression.

Then commonsense intervened and I explained the nature of the 'brick'.

Panic over, on to the bar, have a beer and a smoke.

Ah! 'No Smoking' signs all over the place. I asked at the bar as to where this was permitted and was directed outside of the terminal building to the taxi rank for my nicotine 'fix'.

In the United States at that time passengers in the departure lounge didn't need to negotiate immigration in either direction, only security. So, I wandered out, had my cigarette and returned. There was a different security guard on duty.

'What's this sir?'

'A brick.'

The security guard looked at me with a blank expression.

I then again explained the nature of the 'brick'.

Around half an hour later I was contemplating the nature of 8 to 10 hours without a cigarette and decided to venture, once again, to the taxi rank.

Now I think they must change security guards frequently in California for on my return, yet another guard was there.

'What's this sir?'

'A brick.'

The security guard looked at me with a blank expression.

For the third time I explained the nature of the 'brick'. I must say that by this time I was becoming quite fluent in the patter.

* * *

I think by now that you will have the idea, a good few cigarettes later and one can imagine the next security briefing.

'Anything unusual today?'

'Yessir, there was a limey today trying to smuggle London Bridge back to Ingerland piece by
piece!'

I should add here that no bricks were harmed in the course of this story and that the paving brick was delivered unharmed to the consignee.

CHAPTER 5

Home comforts

Whenever travelling one always relates to home comparing the plumbing, the food, the drink and so on.

I have yet to be convinced that the manufacturers of hotel plumbing equipment do not see a challenge in providing bathroom fittings that visitors are unable to operate.

It is natural to seek commodities which are similar in some way to those found 'chez nous' in order to make the surroundings feel more familiar.

After some experience it is usual to compensate for lack of certain comforts by taking them in luggage. I have on a number of occasions included brown sauce on my packing list of essentials.

On the whole, whilst I have found travelling to be immensely rewarding and pleasurable there really is nothing like getting back to my own bed, especially.....

It was 1986, I was visiting East Africa. My first visit to the region. On my arrival at the hotel I was surprised at the standard of facilities in comparison to those offered by hotels in Europe and the Middle East.

I carried with me a bottle of whisky requested by a business contact at my next port of call. As such I had no alcoholic beverage for personal consumption. Later in life one of my colleagues gave my what I consider to be one of the best pieces of advice, always carry a bottle of whisky for yourself. Not only for personal consumption but it can also be used to open doors.

Anyway, back to the tale. The room I was allocated was to such a low state of repair that I made a list that I would have found difficult to accept elsewhere when one was paying in excess of US $100 per night.

* * *

For your information I reproduce the list:

1. No lock on door.
2. Cockroaches in bathroom.
3. Telephone not working.
4. No lightbulb in bedroom.
5. Neon light tube in bathroom replaced by standard lightbulb, electrical connections selotaped into place.
6. Air-conditioning system not working.
7. Wallpaper around bed filthy and peeling.
8. Bed bugs. (I later found out that the dirty wallpaper was a result of previous guests spraying insect repellent onto it to prevent the bugs! I have to admit that I added to the stains.)

Whilst making this list I felt the need to have a drink. As the aforementioned whisky was for a future contact, I removed myself to the hotel bar. Arriving at the bar I approached the bartender and requested a beer.

'No beer.'
OK, a coke?

'No coke.'

I asked him what he did have.

'Pineapple juice.'

So, I bought a pineapple juice, warm, in a dirty can.

While drinking this a local gentleman went to the bar and purchased a bottle of beer and a coke. I had now finished the, surprisingly refreshing, juice. I returned to the bar and asked for another.

'No pineapple juice.'

By now the penny had dropped.

'What have you got?'

* * *

'Beer.'

Wonderful, at last, 'I'll have a beer.'

'No glasses.'

If you try and fail, try again and fail again, give up. There's no point in being a damn fool about it. I retired from the bar and tried my luck in the restaurant.

Now, bearing in mind the condition of the room and the fact that the hotel bar had no glasses would you expect to be refused entry to the restaurant for not wearing a tie?

I was.

CHAPTER 6

Thinking outside the box

Following on from the previous story a colleague of mine was travelling, again in Africa, when he had the misfortune to be grounded, overnight at an unexpected stop due to aeroplane technical problems.

Offered a free beverage at the hotel bar, courtesy of the airline, he requested a coke.

'Sorry, no coke.' Was the reply.

At the same time a fellow traveller asked for, and received, a whisky and coke.

'Hang on a minute, you just gave him a whisky and coke.'

'Yes.'

But you said you have no coke.'

'That's right sir, only whisky and coke as per the menu.'

'So, can I have a whisky and coke but without the whisky?'

'Sorry sir, that is not possible.'

'OK, so can I have a whisky and coke in separate glasses?'

'Certainly sir.'

My friend got his coke, and the fellow traveller got another whisky, gratis.

Cheers!

CHAPTER 7

Shut that door

I am not exactly a technophobe. I use a pc, I have a mobile phone, a tablet, my car has electric windows.

Electric windows, now there's a tale.

Every year in Duesseldorf there is a medical fair. This fair was usually held in the last week of November. My company attended this fair 'en masse' and due to the high demand for rooms hotels increase their prices accordingly. 'Messe preis' is a common phrase meaning that the price has risen by around 300%. We used to regularly book rooms at a quaint hotel in one of the surrounding towns and drive to the fair in a hire car.

This car would vary year on year depending on the number of people we had to transport.

One year we had a people carrier.

We collected the vehicle at the airport and drove straight to the fairground to set up our stand. On our return we noticed, to our concern, that the front windows were open. Fortunately, no-one had removed our luggage, so we had a cheap lesson. Later we discovered that the front windows opened automatically, some form of safety feature I believe designed to alleviate air pressure in cold climates.

The following evening, I realised that I had left my mobile phone in the vehicle. I opened the door, retrieved my phone and shut the door.

Noticing that the driver's window was open I turned on the ignition and closed it, locking the door as I left.

That night it snowed.

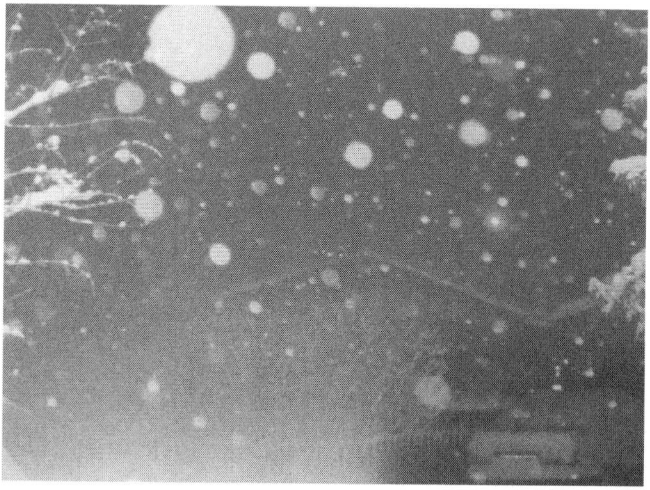

The next morning, we were sitting having breakfast admiring the newly fallen blanket before it turned to that unsightly slush after people have walked and driven through it.

The car parking for the hotel was at the front of the building, right in front of the breakfast room.

One of my colleagues remarked how wonderful it was that the people carrier we were driving had cleared the snow from the front passenger's window. Err….

Sure enough, I had closed the driver's window, but the passengers had also opened and there was a beautiful covering of snow over the passenger's seat.

I was OK, I was the driver.

CHAPTER 8

Follow the Instructions

It has been said that when all else fails, read the instructions.

At secondary school I had a woodwork teacher who treated all pupils as idiots, which we probably were in those days and at that age.

He would give us just one task to do at any one time and then check everyone's work. Often some poor soul would go a stage further than instructed.

When this occurred, the misfortunate would be soundly rapped across the knuckles with the bit of timber he was responsible for.

Very occasionally, if the misdemeanour was sufficient, the timber was applied to the skull of the offending lad.

I should note that this was well before the days of 'PCness' when teachers were permitted to discipline their classes.

I often wonder how that teacher would have reacted had he been the flight attendant on a recent journey in the Middle East.

The flight was not particularly busy, and everyone found their seats easily.

We were sitting on the aircraft, taxiing for take-off when the obligatory safety announcement started.

As per usual the cabin crew stood in the aisle to demonstrate the instructions.

'Please pay attention to the following safety announcement, blah, blah, blah. Your life jacket is under your seat, blah, blah, blah. The life jacket is fitted and tied so. To inflate the life jacket, you pull the toggle as demonstrated …' pppsssssst!

* * *

The flight attendant was ignored as everyone within earshot turned to look where the hissing noise was coming from. A number of rows behind me a small gentleman, who had been avidly listening to, and following, the safety instructions to the letter, was firmly wedged into his seat by the now fully inflated life jacket. His smug smile of satisfaction at having beaten his classmates to the final task was quickly wiped away as he realised that he was the only passenger, not only to have retrieved his life jacked and put it on, but also to have inflated it. Having had her safety demonstration ruined all the flight attendant could do (there were no pieces of wood lying on bench-tops to use to good effect) was to prod the jacket gently with a plastic fork.

CHAPTER 9

You should have gone before we left

Another story from East Africa in the mid eighties.

I was visiting my distributor, his representative and I got on really well and we had lunch at a marvellous restaurant on the edge of a game reserve just outside Nairobi serving very exotic meats. At the end of the meal, the lunch having concluded the days' business, my host proposed that we pay a brief visit to the game reserve on the way back to the hotel, saying that lions were known to reside there and if we were really lucky we might spot a pride of them.

This sounded a wonderful idea for someone who had only ever seen some of these magnificent animals in captivity.

To set the scene KC, as I knew him, drove a battered old Peugeot 504 which, by his own admission, was held together by chewing gum and plasters.

This was not unusual in Kenya in those days as lack of foreign currency led to a shortage of imported goods which in turn led to some innovative practices.

The game reserve covers 45 square miles with one open side allowing wildlife to enter and roam at will. Not only lions but buffalo, rhino, cheetahs, baboons, hippopotami, gazelle and impala are common sights.

Rangers are few and far between and if the vehicle broke down in those days one relied on the car horn, mobile phones were far in the future.

We had not long seen a pride of lions when KC decided that after the heavy lunch with copious amounts of the local Tusker beer, he needed to relieve himself.

* * *

At this stage I must say the KC was capable of drinking a Tusker beer faster than I could pay for it.

For him to have five or six in half an hour was not unusual. In addition, these were the days before drink driving was socially frowned upon.

In the middle of a 45 square mile game reserve, nothing man-made to see at all, less than a mile from a pride of wild lions he calmly opened the car door.

'I won't be a minute' he said.

I wasn't quite so confident.

"Be sure to leave the car keys in the ignition" I instructed, 'and should anything happen, I'll see you back at the hotel."

CHAPTER 10

Who's that man?

It was Summer 1989, and I was visiting Zurich with a colleague. We had a particularly tiring day and I arrived at my hotel around 7 in the evening. (My colleague was staying with a friend). Unfortunately, due to the late arrival time the hotel had given my reserved room to another guest. However the law in Switzerland is that a reserved room must be honoured, even if the hotel has to find a room in a more expensive establishment the customer only pays the agreed price and the difference is sorted out between the two hotels.

On this particular day there was an athletics meeting in Zurich and the only room available was at the Hotel Baur Au Lac, at that time one of if not THE most expensive hotel in Zurich.

Who was I to argue at being offered one of the most expensive rooms in Zurich at a very reasonable price?

Checking in with the usual formalities; registration card, passport etc. I couldn't help but notice a powerfully built, tallish, black gentleman surrounded by another 4 similarly built gentlemen who were at least 6 inches taller and displaying great deference to the former.

They were quietly going about their business, but it was evident that they were minders for the first gentleman.

Being British one does not make a scene but as he was leaving, I asked the concierge who he was.

Looking at me in amazement the concierge said, "do you not recognize the fastest man in the World (at that time) six Olympic gold medal winner?" I had to admit my ignorance as athletics was not one of my favoured pastimes …

…"Carl Lewis".

Well at least he wasn't being accompanied by Clint Eastwood!

CHAPTER 11

They never show that in films

For my sins and to the chagrin of medical professionals I am a lifelong smoker.

I have tried many times to give up the dreaded weed, but it is one thing I have found myself unable to do without.

It is also one vice which is currently legal in all countries, unlike alcohol.

Believe me I have suffered as a result of this. I have never been on the upper deck of a Boeing 747 for example and being made to feel a pariah is quite common. "Those who must, now may."

There was, however, one time where my addiction proved not only acceptable but downright useful.

Mid/late 1990's I was in Melbourne visiting my distributor there, a lovely lady with a real 'action man' partner. He didn't smoke, drink or chase women. Where he got his 'kicks' was with adrenaline. A great white shark reported in Melbourne harbour would send him out on his jet ski to get a close encounter with the creature. His ride-on lawnmower was tuned to allow racing around his garden. When the thrill there faded there was always his 350 horsepower Holden Monaro. I am sure that you understand the type.

On this particular visit I was spending the weekend in Melbourne with my distributor. Her partner, let's call him Graham, proposed that he, one of his colleagues and I go away for the weekend to indulge in a little male bonding. Why not, I thought, nothing can go too amiss.

Wrong

Graham's idea of male bonding was to take a Toyota Landcruiser to a place called Woods Point, a wonderful town, population c94 in 1996, around 110 miles Northeast of Melbourne in the Great Dividing Range where one of his friends, a Professor at Melbourne University, mined gold in his spare time. At that time the authorities allowed claims to be staked on mines providing they were 'worked'.

The accommodation was a small shack in the woods, with bedrooms added by pushing the back halves of trucks in the side of the shell and sealing the holes. The Professor was teaching at this time and so the place was at our disposal.

Electricity was supplied via a generator, there was running cold water, I never found out from where, and the 'dunny' was a bench outside with a hole cut into it, over a pit, with the most wonderful open air views.

Being the only smoker, I was constantly being ribbed over my unhealthy habit.

We went in the winter and so wildlife activity; snakes, possums etc. was thankfully at a minimum although we did have to be wary about hibernating creatures.

We bought provisions from the local store and the first day explored the ore processing; belts for sifting and sorting together with the machinery which crushed the raw material. This was an absolutely fascinating experience, especially when considering that it was all operated by one man.

The next day we went down the mine itself, a very unnerving experience as crowd control fences had been used for ladders, and tried our skills at motorbike riding. The other two were experienced riders, this was my first, and only, motorcycle experience although I must say I found it thrilling, terrifying, exhilarating and rewarding in equal measures. Oh, I almost forgot, painful too as I managed to break one of my metatarsal bones in the process.

The day over we returned to base where it was noticed that I had a foreign object on my neck, a leech.

Examination established that Graham and his colleague also had uninvited visitors attached to them.

Now at the time we unanimously acknowledged that the best way to disturb these 'friends' was to heat the body, causing discomfort to the leach and thus encouraging it to remove its' head from the wound and allow removal of the whole body without leaving any part to cause infection.

As I have said before I was the only smoker.

I regally rolled a cigarette, lit it and passed it around our small group and one by one the unwelcome parasites were safely removed.

Just one thing though, in 'The African Queen' Humphrey Bogart removed leeches in this fashion and that was the end of it.

In real life, due to the anti-coagulent injected to assist blood flow, one can ruin a perfectly good shirt.

They never show that in films.

CHAPTER 12

Take your purchases and go!

In UK it is common practice to have price tags on nearly all items for sale in shops. The main exceptions being product sold by weight and even then, there is usually a price per kilo to compare. With few exceptions customers are expected to respect these prices.

In other countries the barter system exists where customers are expected to haggle a little. Foreigners are usually quoted an extraordinarily high price so that a little more can be taken from the original offer and still afford a handsome profit for the retailer.

It can take some time to get used to this system to ensure that a fair price is paid whilst at the same time not allowing the bargaining 'bug' to bite too hard. I remember once refusing the purchase of a very reasonable leather briefcase because the vendor was not prepared to discuss the price, well it was an airport duty free shop. Something I later regretted.

This barter system covers everything from negotiating the price of a non-metered fare with a taxi driver, to the cost of a fake Rolex with a hawker on the beach and on to goods supplied by a humble shopkeeper.

Ah, the humble shopkeeper…

Mumbai, around 1998, I was participating at an exhibition being held in the World Trade Centre.

The World Trade Centre in Mumbai in an impressive building complex consisting of two towers which, at that time, was the tallest building in South Asia.

The exhibition was taking place on one of the lower floors and was a fairly dreary affair.

During one of the lulls in business I took the opportunity to explore other parts of the building and came across a mini shopping centre on the ground or lower floor.

One of the shops was a clothes shop which was what can best be described as 'busy' with fabrics and garments strewn all over the place.

I entered and was pounced on by the proprietor. I explained that I was considering the purchase of a few shawls, gifts for the ladies back in the office.

Within two seconds a selection of different coloured shawls was removed from their hiding place and grandiosely displayed in their full glory on the sales counter.

Seeing that I was not already reaching for my wallet the zealous vendor decided to overwhelm me with a further display of yet more colours and patterns, grandly strewn over the former selection.

Despite my protests the eager host decided to display a further handful of shawls.

By this time there were around 30 shawls on the counter.

* * *

How many did I require? Around 10, however it would depend on the cost.

Looking me up and down to gauge my wealth the shopkeeper hesitated, made a few calculations on a pocket calculator (for effect) and gave me a figure for all 10 shawls.

Not saying a word, I theatrically made a note of the price in a notebook, expressed my thanks, turned and walked out of the store, saying that I would return later.

The following day, during another lull in proceedings, I took the opportunity to revisit my newfound friend.

The shawls, which had been carefully refolded and put away after my previous visit were again displayed with a flourish and a request as to which I would like to buy.

I took out my notebook and again asked how much. The response this time was similar to the first; calculator out, finger poking the keys, head scratching and followed by pained facial expression and the offer of a price a little lower than the previous day.

I too re-enacted my actions of the day before, taking out my notebook, noting the new price and bidding my farewell with the promise that I would return later.

The exhibition ran for 3 days. I made several more visits to the shop, each time with a repeat scenario. Each time leaving with a slightly lower price.

The final day I went in, bought the items, paid a price a little higher than the last price he had offered me, thanked him for his time and dodged the parcel of 10 shawls which had been launched at my head …

CHAPTER 13

Oh, the quaint days of yore

Visiting Jerusalem with one of my colleagues we spent a few hours touring the Old City.

As forewarned from events in a previous chapter we avoided the hawkers, enjoyed a cold beer in a bar adjacent to the Wailing Wall and on leaving the city we saw a sight which took me back to what seemed like time immemorial.

Picture this: the old cobbled, narrow streets; high stone walls, bleached in the unrelenting sun over thousands of years; a cloudless sky; the sun beating down; totally unspoiled views over the Garden of Gethsemane with the Mount of Olives serenely magnificent in the background; traders busying themselves moving their wares to more advantageous positions; nothing man-made in view from since BC; a very aged man in traditional arab dress sitting on his camel.

We felt as if we had been transported back two thousand years.

'What a moment,' exclaimed my colleague, 'all we need is a Roman Centuria to pass by and the picture would be complete.'

I absent-mindedly agreed as I contemplated where my next cold beer was coming from.

Then the scenario developed, although not as we expected.

Following my colleague's comments, the aged man on the camel dropped his right hand, hitched up his long khaki coloured robe and answered his mobile telephone ...

Two thousand years of romance died in a split second.

CHAPTER 14

It can't be that hot, can it?

One thing that is evident when travelling abroad is that culinary tastes are very different.

This is probably one of the main cultural differences which travellers of all kinds are first aware of.

For example, in Mediterranean countries the temperature food is served at is often much lower than that in more northern climes. Many cultures have seriously spiced food whereas others may have relatively bland tastes. Everything is relative and dependent on climate and outside cultural influences over the centuries.

I am not referring to the type of food, that will come in a later story, I refer to the differences in standard presentations according to the origin of the chef so that, if a steak is ordered medium/well done in UK it is somewhat longer cooked than with a similar instruction in France.

It is well known that most food claiming to be Indian served in the UK is prepared by chefs from Bangladesh. To truly experience Indian food, one should travel to the region in India relative to the dish. The popular Balti dish is widely believed to have originated in Birmingham, although the word 'balti' is from Northern Pakistan as the steel or iron pot in which the food is cooked.

Now Indian food particularly is one where I have found a vast difference in the preparation and taste dependant on the country I have dined in. This type of food lends itself very well to being adjusted to suit local tastes. Many descriptions familiar to us in UK are totally alien in other countries, even India, just as some traditional Indian dishes are alien to us in UK. For example, who has tried the delicious 'dum pukht'? More often than not the level of spices is reduced to suit more refined tastes.

* * *

Now the heathens which I have had the dubious pleasure to travel with often befriend the waiter and negotiate a slightly 'hotter' presentation.

The most spectacular account of this took place in early 1990's in the Frankfurt region of Germany.

My company at that time took part in an exhibition and I booked a hotel through a friend of mine who lived in the area. We numbered around 10 people.

A few of us arrived early to set up the exhibition and to our delight we found that the small town we were staying in had an Indian restaurant. Not only an Indian restaurant but, at that time, the ONLY Indian restaurant in Hesse, the Frankfurt region.

On his arrival and being informed of this the smile on the Sales Director's face promised great things for my career. I was promised the moon as we ate there nearly every night,

until …

The penultimate evening, the Managing Director, the Big Cheese, the Head Honcho, came over to view the exhibition and to see what we were up to. He decided to come out with us for dinner.

Everyone being fully aware that his experience of 'piquant' food was almost non-existent he was encouraged to order a somewhat bland chicken dish.

After 3 or 4 mouthfuls of his Chicken Korma, plus quite a few German beers both before and during the meal our Managing Director now considered himself an expert in Indian cuisine, quite prepared to try other, more adventurous dishes.

What better idea than to try the Sales Directors' chicken vindaloo, which the waiter had been instructed to 'beef up' a little with the words "may I try some?"

With no hesitation and without awaiting a reply he took a large spoonful of the vindaloo, mainly sauce with a small piece of chicken and shovelled it into his mouth.

A lull ensued, followed by the hiss of steam leaving his ears, tears running down his cheeks, gasping and voiceless pointing vigorously from his mouth to the jug of water on the table.

Sympathy to his situation was shown by all at the table once the tears of laughter and the aching bellies had been addressed.

The only beneficiary of this tasting was the local water board as demand in the State of Hesse over that one evening surpassed a normal month.

I believe that, on return to 'Blighty' the unfortunate man employed the services of a maxillo-facial surgeon to reconstruct what was left of his mouth, the careers of both the Sales Director and I went immediately rock-bottom and the closest I got to the moon was looking at it through my window.

CHAPTER 15

How to travel on a budget

Japan is expensive. In November 1994 my company exhibited at an international congress in Kobe. This was to be my first visit to Japan and a great deal of research was made to ensure that I understood the local business customs and picked up a few polite words. On researching the costs involved, hotels, transport etc. I also decided that we would make a concerted effort to use the exercise to make contact with commercial partners.

At that time assistance and advice was available from all corners for commercial trade with Japan. I duly spent the six months prior to the exhibition diligently establishing contacts to meet during the congress.

The plan was that I would fly into Kobe as part of a Far East tour I was doing at the time. A colleague would join me, flying direct from UK and we would at some time be joined by the co-owner of the company with his family who were visiting primarily for sightseeing.

As such the co-owner made his own travel and accommodation arrangements whilst I sorted out my colleague and myself.

These were the days before the internet, there were no reviews or photographs of the interior and the most expedient way of arranging accommodation was via a large reference book of all registered hotels in the area which gave just price indication and address with contact details. No e-mails, the reservation had to be made by telex or fax. Combined with a map to ascertain the convenience of the accommodation in relation to the congress centre and travel to and from the airport this reference book assisted the selection of our rooms for the week.

On my arrival the hotel looked OK, clean, smart and with incredibly polite staff.

I note here that in Japan tipping is not an accepted custom, taxi drivers will insist on giving the correct change and hotel porters expect no gratuity, indeed, they would be offended should one be offered.

The room was not the largest room in which I have stayed, in fact I would estimate that the entire 'suite' was no bigger than 2.5 x 2.5 metres, including the shower room. I experimented and found that I was almost able to touch opposite walls at the same time. However, it would suffice.

I then left the hotel to explore the surroundings and find something to eat.

Within a short walk of the hotel was a restaurant complex.

In Japan great consideration is given to foreigners who do not understand the language. Traditional restaurants have their menu dishes replicated in realistic plastic on display in the window with prices allowing one to have a good idea of what to order.

In some of the better-looking restaurants the prices were considerably higher than I thought my expenses budget would allow and so I had a reasonable, if somewhat bland, curry in a lower cost establishment.

The following day my colleague arrived, and we dined at the same place wondering if we would be surviving on the bare minimum for the duration.

The stand at the exhibition proved to be in the perfect spot, visible from the entrance and easily found. The co-owner, his wife and son visited on the first day. They were pleased by the effort that had been put into the display and the result. They invited us for dinner that evening at their hotel.

When travelling on business I always consider the value for money aspect with regards to expenditure vs outcome. At that time the company I worked for was a small player in the market with a solid financial base and careful with money.

The hotel the co-owner was staying at was part of an international chain, sited at the main railway station some 30 minutes' walk from our hotel.

* * *

This was not a cheap hotel.

We arrived at the appointed time and met the co-owner in the bar with his family. We then migrated to the restaurant where we were served Kobe beef in the teppanyaki grill.

Now if you are not vegetarian and have never eaten Kobe beef you have missed out on one of life's treats, it is superb. However, the cost is at the top end of the price spectrum.

After this magnificent feast we retired to the sports bar of the hotel where we were treated to copious amounts of beer whilst we demonstrated the finer arts of playing pool to a group of Americans.

In the following days we were treated to this delicacy a number of times and on one occasion my Australian distributor joined us with a friend.

All these meals were on the account of the co-owner of the company and who were we to argue?

However, the gruelling schedule of being up early, attending the exhibition all day to go out in the evening and arriving back to our rooms late took its' toll and so on the fourth day, of five, we proposed that we entertain ourselves for the evening and allow the co-owner to have some spare time.

On the final night, fully refreshed from our quiet evening we once again joined the owner and his family for a last supper.

Being the final evening, we again ate Kobe beef and returned to our lodgings in the early hours of the morning, rising early to checkout and meet the co-owner at his hotel at the railway station.

We arrived just as he was checking himself and his family out.

I went up to the counter to greet him and noticed he was a little subdued, mumbling about how he was going to be able to justify the expenses to his more frugal partner. My eyes strayed to the counter and I understood his demeanour.

* * *

The final bill for his week at the hotel: rooms, meals, drinks and excursions came well into 5 figures in US$ approaching the average annual salary in UK at that time.

Still, it was probably the very best I have ever eaten over a week and certainly better than if I had been left to my own devices.

And I underspent my budget ...

CHAPTER 16

Six bills, one beer and one coffee

Throughout the World waiters are the same.

Their World is their domain. Diners are only sent to cause upheaval to their beautifully placed settings, challenge their knowledge of the speciality dishes and provide tips.

Experienced waiters will identify who is the senior diner at the table as they are the ones most likely to be paying the bill and therefore determining the gratuity.

My colleagues and I visited a highly recommended traditional restaurant in Germany. There were seven of us and although we had no reservation there was sufficient spare table space for us to be seated immediately.

Our waiter was a little aged, certainly well past retirement age and this added to the charm of the place.

Being the only German speaker at the table I dutifully translated my colleagues' requirements for starters and mains, together with their beverage wishes.

These were carefully entered into a hand-held terminal the waiter carried which he then pointed at a receiver somewhere in the restaurant to transmit our order to the relevant back of house personnel.

For clarity there were seven of us. We ordered six starters, seven main courses and seven drinks.

The waiter departed and a few moments later returned with the ordered drinks.

A few minutes later he returned with seven starters. He was a little confused that we only wanted six and so we agreed to have the seven he served to us, the abstainer, me, agreeing to suffer in the cause of détente.

The empty dishes cleared away the waiter then brought six main courses …

It had been a long, hard day and I set about explaining to the old codger that we actually required another main course. This was difficult because I believe his hearing aid batteries were beyond their useful life.

Eventually the seventh main was delivered and the final diner, me, ate in silence alone much to the mirth of my colleagues.

Dinner over it was agreed that six wanted coffee, one another beer and due to the slow service, we would ask for the bill at the same time.

This was too much for our elderly host who repeated the order as six bills, one coffee and one beer.

I patiently corrected him, and the beverages were duly and accurately brought to the table.

Then the bill arrived ... for six coffees and one beer ... that's all folks!

CHAPTER 17

Never use your left hand

1986, and one of my first visits to the Middle East. The last port of call was Amman, Jordan.

Having worked in London for a mineral exploration outfit based in Saudi Arabia in a previous life I was aware of a number of customs in this part of the World. One of which was that the use of the left hand was to be avoided as it is regarded as unclean.

Should you require an explanation of this then I suggest that you look up a reference book.

My day commenced in an unsettling manner as I waited in the hotel lobby for my appointment. The reception of the hotel was suddenly full.

Fifty or so men brandishing Kalashnikov assault rifles were ambling around the concourse.

They did not appear to have a hostile demeanour, and no one seemed intimidated by them.

I enquired of the concierge as to their purpose to be informed that the Palestinian Liberation Organisation had a meeting there that day.

Oh well, I might as well go out ...

My business contact there was a very highly respected local businessman and after our affairs were concluded he very kindly invited me to lunch. However, he did explain that this would be as his guest at a Rotary Club meeting.

Undaunted I eagerly accepted the invitation as I was not only hungry but also interested in the machinations of a Rotary Club meeting.

* * *

The meeting started with a long, long, long presentation on the Arab/ Israeli six-day war of 1967 with diagrams and pictures explaining the mistakes made.

The presentation was interminable although it probably didn't last for more than two hours.

But it was conducted wholly in Arabic.

Then the meal came.

I am left-handed.

The first course was tomato soup.

My shirt WAS white.

But I didn't use my left hand.

CHAPTER 18

The Rabbit and the Slug

At the end of the 20th Century company cars were very popular as vehicles were relatively expensive compared to salaries. They really were regarded as status symbols and the choice of company car was a very emotional issue. Comparing unfavourable specifications with others in the same department caused much discontent within organizations.

It is unbelievable how the suffixes 'L'. 'GL', 'GLS' 'Ghia' and 'SRi', combined with electric front (and possibly rear) windows, sunroof, tachometer, rear seat pockets and electric wing mirrors were so emotive that they were regarded as part of the whole salary package used to entice executives from one company to another.

Every company had a car policy, and these varied dramatically depending on a number of, now irrelevant, factors.

At one company I worked for I inherited a Ford Sierra 1.6GL from my predecessor, a reasonable spec'd car by the standards of the day, not looking too shabby in the drive although not the Ghia spec which would really have impressed the neighbours.

This particular vehicle had the misfortune to have been made at the change from leaded to unleaded petrol. At the time Ford insisted that engine components could withstand the lack of lead in the fuel providing that once in every four fills leaded petrol was used.

I don't think my predecessor read that part of the instructions …

This thing could not maintain the national speed limit when climbing a slight incline on the motorway. It was impossible to red line the tachometer with the vehicle in gear and the acceleration could possibly have put a Citroen 2CV to shame although I never found one going slow enough to try this out.

* * *

Everyone in the company called the car 'the Slug'.

This car was used for extensive transport within Europe which was my area of responsibility in those days. Mainly France, a pleasant drive from Calais, using the Route Peripherique in Paris to slingshot west towards Rouen, turning off at Orgeval where our distributor was based and a lovely hotel on the banks of the river Seine.

On the return the car was usually loaded up with beer and wine, increasing the axle weight and causing a further deterioration in performance.

I should note here that, considering the clapped-out engine, this was the first car in which I was ever caught speeding.

Our Managing Director, as befitted his station in life, had a BMW525i.

He was very proud of this car because he could achieve 150 mph in it on any road he liked to, legally or otherwise, usually otherwise.

It was some experience to travel with him driving on a German autobahn at 150 mph (to be clear that is approximately 250 kph) in driving rain, 3 feet (one metre) away from the car in front trying to hold a coherent conversation with him whilst all the time evaluating the survival changes of exiting the vehicle at that speed.

I have confirmed statements of occasions his travelling companions contemplated evacuating the vehicle whilst still in motion.

There were a number of us at a congress in Frankfurt. The final day lots were drawn as to who would be with the Managing Director for the return drive to UK and who would accompany me in the only alternative, the Slug.

The first leg of the drive was a comfortable 300 miles from Frankfurt to Zeebrugge from where our ferry was departing.

Both cars departed at the same time, the BMW speeding off in a cloud of rubbery smoke, the Slug being delayed whilst attempting to outpace a dustcart.

* * *

We assumed that would be the last we saw of the BMW until we arrived at Zeebrugge and we were correct.

What we were completely incorrect over was the time our colleagues would have to wait for us after their white-knuckle ride through Germany, Holland and Belgium.

The Managing Director had decided to demonstrate the superiority of his car over that of his subordinate, stopping only to refuel or for comfort breaks.

He duly arrived at the rendezvous point anticipating a lengthy wait.

Speechless was not a sufficient description when he saw the Slug arrive no later than 15 minutes after him.

The lower speed led to far superior fuel economy and no need for stops on the leisurely five-hour journey. The 'Slug' had redeemed itself.

CHAPTER 19

Make me happy

As mentioned in an earlier chapter bartering, or bargaining, is commonplace in many countries.

The seller quotes an exceptionally high price; the buyer returns with a much lower offer; the seller complains about the cost of living and his starving children, he then lowers the price a little; the buyer looks despairingly into his wallet and then ups his offer; and so on and so forth.

Eventually the two parties reach an agreement, in most cases at a price favourable to the vendor and the buyer obtains the product he requires.

Everybody is happy.

Happy, now there is a word. It is the word that I fear most of all in any bartering situation.

It has no value, it is not measured in 10's, 100's or 1,000's, it just is.

For example, in a shop you ask the man behind the counter how much is a bar of chocolate. You expect to receive the reply in a number and the currency so that you are aware the chocolate costs, say, one pound.

Instead you receive the response 'make me happy'.

What does this mean? Do you start by offering what you know is a ridiculously low coin expecting the shopkeeper to laugh?

Or do you offer payment of approximately the value you think it should be?

Believe me, offering payment higher than the true value will result in it being quickly accepted, perhaps even grudgingly as the recipient had hoped for more.

You will never know.

* * *

This issue is exacerbated when discussing payment for a service against which there is nothing to gauge the value.

A guide offers to show you the pyramids of the Valley of the Kings at Heliopolis just on the outskirts of Cairo.

Before starting you ask him the price.

'Make me happy' he says.
'But how much?'
'Not a lot, just make me happy.'

At this point one has only two choices.

One… Find another guide

OR

Two… Get royally ripped off

* * *

It's your choice, you cannot say I haven't warned you.

CHAPTER 20

But it's still moving

Since 1994 I have spent a great deal of time in Japan. As you will read in the postscript it was a visit here that stimulated the idea of this book.

There are many incredible wonders here in a country that was for centuries completely isolated from the World. Being an island has its advantages and one should note that the Japanese feel spiritually close to the British, both nations being isolated from any other landmass.

Although our cultures are oppositely opposed the Japanese understand the development of our culture due to the geophysical insulation we have in common with them.

The first visit is always a culture shock. Taxi drivers wear white gloves and caps; the nearside rear door is remotely controlled by the driver; most designs are with space saving in mind; two tier parking spaces and two tier bicycle racks are just a few that come to mind.

When you see Japanese tourists taking photographs of what we consider to be mundane things remember that they are as bemused by our designs as we are of theirs.

I have become acquainted with a number of the customs, but food can be an issue.

I have tried many local delicacies including crocodile, deep fried chicken feet, shark fin soup, goat's intestine and sheep's brain. Most of them I have tried with gusto and although I would not go out of my way to have them, they complimented the setting in which they were served.

I do, however, like my meat cooked and raw dishes, such as sushi or steak tartare, I tend to avoid whenever possible.

* * *

On one of my earlier visits to Japan I was taken to a traditional restaurant and was working out how to shell the prawns on my plate using the chopsticks provided.

Seeing my dilemma my local contact demonstrated by picking up a whole prawn and taking the complete body, shell, legs and head, into his mouth and ate everything.

My colleague on I were on a tour of Japan, starting at Kyoto and ending up in Tokyo, taking the bullet train passing Mount Fuji en route.

Our business contacts were excellent hosts and in Kyoto we had been treated to pufferfish, a delicacy which can be lethal if not prepared correctly. I understand that chefs train for many years before they are allowed to 'go solo' and prepare the fish for human consumption without the supervision of an experienced overseer.

As I am still living, at the time of writing, I can say that it is a delightful dish.

In Tokyo another contact kindly invited us to another traditional restaurant.

On arrival we removed our shoes and sat at a table where there were no chairs, merely a pit in which to place our legs whilst we sat on the floor.

Customary drinks were ordered, and our host ordered from the menu.

The meal consisted of different small course, each one more traditional than the former.

The final serving was the 'piece de resistance', a good-sized uncooked flatfish lying on its' side, sliced along the same direction as the gills.

The host with his chopsticks took a slice and placed it reverently on my colleagues' plate. He then repeated the exercise for he and I.

My colleague sat, staring at the main body of the fish, mouth agape and looking decidedly ill at ease.

He excused himself to visit the little boys' room. On his return he gesticulated discretely to me to draw my attention to the fact that the fish being served was fresh.

So fresh in fact that it was still alive and moving on the plate.

Having researched the subject I can find no word for a non-fish eater, but I became one that evening.

CHAPTER 21

Have a quiet drink

Another topic on personal safety when travelling.

I am often asked about the most beautiful city I have visited, the friendliest, the warmest, the coldest and the most dangerous.

I must say that in the last category Sao Paulo wins in the Southern Hemisphere whilst New Orleans takes the honours in the Northern Hemisphere.

I am talking here about safety under normal, everyday conditions, not safety which has been compromised through conflict or terrorism.

Regular travel teaches one to be cautious, not making overt demonstrations of wealth and taking care if walking streets after dark.

Occasionally though even the most seasoned traveller drops a clanger …

I had flown from Melbourne to New Orleans, crossing the dateline in the 'wrong' direction so that after a tiringly long journey I actually arrived earlier than I took off.

This being my first visit here the hotel had been proposed by our Managing Director as he was particularly partial to one of the rooms. To this day I know not why, perhaps it suited his colonial background.

The hotel whilst pleasant enough had no bar but it was only one block from Bourbon Street, the famous tourist part of New Orleans which was full of hostelries.

Bourbon Street, like the Zona Rosa in Mexico City, has a high police presence, mainly I believe for the protection of tourists. In fact, there is probably a horse mounted officer on every street corner. This presence is restricted only to Bourbon Street and it is locally acknowledged that the further one gets away from the main drag the less advisable it is to walk.

I had noticed on my arrival at the hotel that just 50 metres walk down the street was a bar / diner.

Only requiring a few beers and something to allay my hunger, being around 8.30 in the evening, I wandered down to the diner and ordered my beer and a burger, sitting at an empty table.

When I entered the establishment there were probably around 20 men there of mixed Caucasian, Afro-American and Hispanic backgrounds a jovial crew in good humour.

The refreshments duly arrived, and I ate my meal then ordered another beer.

To entertain myself I was reading an old English newspaper I had acquired at one of the airports I had passed through.

Well time, and beer, flowed quickly and around four hours later I rose from my seat and approached the bartender to settle the bill.

The bartender informed me that there was a problem with my credit card.

Bemused I followed him to the till behind a screen where I was informed that there was nothing wrong with the card but the bartender wanted to warn me that a great deal of attention was being paid to me, being both a stranger and a foreigner. He felt that I should perhaps take a taxi back to the hotel as he didn't believe that I would make the 50 metres unmolested and with my wallet.

The effect of the five or so beers evaporated as I slowly inspected the fellow inhabitants of the bar.

The number was down to around 10 by this time but the demeanour had changed noticeably and there was no good humour amongst them.

* * *

Looks were averted as I scanned the room, raising my suspicion that perhaps I was the focal point of their attention.

For whatever reason I probably had around US $500 in my wallet and I certainly didn't want to lose that in one go. Remember the dreaded Company Accountant in an earlier chapter?

I visited the dunny, sorry, forgot I was in USA, the restroom and stuffed $450 into the bottom of my sock.

Leaving the restroom, I exclaimed that I would have one final beer and addressing the room asked if anyone would join me. Without waiting for a response, I slammed the $50 note on the counter and instructed the barman to 'fill them up', remarking loudly and with regret that this note was the last of my cash.

Finishing my beer, I walked out of the bar and straight to my hotel unchallenged.

CHAPTER 22

Be careful out there

Following on from the previous chapter it was early 2000's and I was introducing a new colleague to South America.

We were in Sao Paulo and it was the first time my colleague had left the European continent.

As in most places a little caution and common sense is necessary to keep out of unwanted situations.

Sao Paulo is the second most populous city in South and Central America after Mexico City.

On my first visit there some years earlier I had been comprehensively warned by staff at the British Consulate over the issue of personal security: never walk alone or display cash, jewellery, mobile phone or camera.

Indeed, on the journey from the airport to the hotel in the morning rush hour one was offered a wide range of photographic equipment, much of it still loaded with half-used film.

This warning was hammered home by the hotel offering armoured limousines for transfer to the airport to avoid hijacking and the owner of the ubiquitous local Irish bar offering the use of his armed bodyguard to escort a group of us back to the hotel.

Anyway, back to the present (as it was in those days).

Prior to our departure I had briefed my young colleague as to the dos and don'ts of personal security to the extent that his eyes had glazed over with that far away look and the constant 'yes, yes, yes' which indicated that he understood the message and that any further reiteration of the need for caution was superfluous to requirements.

* * *

On arrival at the hotel my colleague was quite cheerful, pointing out that we had seen nothing untoward and insinuating that I was just an old fusspot who over-exaggerated everything and that he felt as safe as he did when walking down his local high street.

I shrugged my shoulders and smiled.

We got into the taxi and started towards our first appointment.

On the second corner, not two minutes drive from the hotel we passed what had been the shootout from a bank raid.

Four body-shaped mounds covered in tarpaulins lay on the pavement next to our taxi.

For the rest of the week my every word of advice was avidly listened to.

On a similar note a year or so later the same colleague was travelling alone in South Africa. He was staying at a hotel in Sandton in the suburbs of Johannesburg.

He called me and sounded a little rattled.

'There has been a shooting in the shopping mall attached to the hotel.' He said, 'What advice do you have?'

Only one thing to say really ...

'Don't go shopping.'

CHAPTER 23

Damen und Herren

It is acknowledged that languages are related. The constant migration and conquering of territories have led to many languages having common words, particularly in modern, technological parlance.

Some words can be, however, a little confusing, especially when crossing multi-cultures.

The scenario is a company dinner in Germany. The German host, some six or seven Brits and an American. The American was a frequent visitor to UK but this was his first ever visit to Germany.

The meal went well, and the wine flowed. The food and company were of a high standard and everyone was winding down with coffee. Our colleague from the other side of the pond rose, declared he had to 'go to the john' and sauntered off.

After some time one of our party went to check on him as we were all concerned over the time it had taken him to commit an act of micturition, wash his hands and return.

From the other side of the door he assured the enquirer he was fine.

Some while later he returned looking somewhat perplexed and bemused.

We challenged him on the time it had taken for this visit and his reply floored us.

'Waaaaaaal, I couldn't decipher the figures on the doors, and one said 'hers' and so I went in the 'da men' door but there were women in there!'

In all fairness to our trans-atlantic friend I have to say that the signage on the doors was a little ambiguous.

It's a funny old World!

Or was it?

CHAPTER 24

Tea or Coffee?

A young lady I have known for many years would not forgive me for omitting this story.

Or perhaps she will not forgive me for including it.

There is only one way to tell.

It is not uncommon at exhibitions throughout the World where there is a dedicated British contingent for local and sometimes imported dignitaries to make an appearance during the course of the show to promote trade and goodwill.

Over the year's members of the Royal Family, Ambassadors, Trade Attaches plus Cabinet Ministers have graced exhibition halls Worldwide, visiting British pavilions and exchanging pleasantries with the hoi polloi.

The visits are usually arranged well in advance and are viewed by exhibitors as an appreciation of their work. These visits also provide the companies selected for personal interaction the opportunity for photo-shoots to raise their profile.

As British pavilions have a corporate sponsor, usually a Trade Association, present organizing the day to day operation of the pavilion these V.I.P's start their visits with the sponsor who then guides them around the pavilion.

For this reason, it is best to keep on the right side of the sponsor.

Here's how not to do it.

At this particular exhibition we were honoured by the visit of the then Minister for Health.

* * *

The Minister was duly shown around the pavilion by the young lady I mentioned at the beginning of this chapter and pre-selected companies were spoken to, their products discussed, and photographs taken.

Later that day a number of us were at the coffee station kindly provided by the sponsor. The coffee station consisted of a bar and a number of tables with stools intended to provide sanctuary from the hordes of visitors or a semi-private meeting area.

The young lady, let's call her Debbie, was full of her visitor, who by all accounts had a successful and enjoyable visit.

After a while Debbie, to emphasize the intimacy of her new acquaintance said, 'and as I said to the Minister this morning ...'

Someone, it certainly was not me, it could not possibly have been me.

Wait, it was me, interjected with, 'tea or coffee?'

No dignitaries were ever introduced to me again.

CHAPTER 25

Anything to Declare?

It is well known that H.M. Customs & Excise, as they used to be called, had a range of powers unique to their arsenal.

For example, a search warrant in UK for a police force details the precise address whereas for HM C & E a range of addresses may be entered under the same warrant.

With reasonable suspicion, whatever that is, a motor vehicle can be dismantled into individual components in an inspection warehouse. Should nothing of interest be found these part will be returned to the owner of the vehicle unassembled.

At the same time, being Civil Servants, they are mainly, if not solely, answerable to their Government Minister. Therefore, any complaints go through a drawn-out procedure which can take many years to process.

It does not pay to take liberties with these guys.

This takes me back to the late 1990's. I was working for a medical company and my work entailed frequent visits in the company car to mainland Europe in order to visit various customers.

Over a period of eighteen months I had probably made some twenty trips from Dover to France and back again.

At around about the fifteenth visit my return arrivals started to become a little unnerving as apparently the frequency of trips had raised flags of suspicion as to the true reason for travel.

I was selected for increasingly intrusive questioning with regards to the reasons for my trips but as I had legitimate reasons, I was not particularly worried, until ...

* * *

The twentieth visit, I took the car to participate at a congress relating to the diabetic foot as my company had recently launched a new product specifically relating to this condition.

The three-day congress was taking place just south of Amsterdam and on the way, I passed by my distributor in Brussels, overnighting there.

The car was packed with luggage for four nights and the sundry paraphernalia required for a congress; samples, brochures, posters and four large spongy feet, These feet measured approximately 100 x 40 x 30 cm but due to the nature of their construction they were sufficiently pliable to fit anywhere in the vehicle.

At the end of the congress, which was midday on a Saturday, I duly packed the car ready for the dash to Calais for the Chunnel home.

The spongy feet were the last to be packed. They were crammed in the boot on top of the luggage, samples and brochures which I had remaining.

With a little persuasion the boot lid closed on the feet.

The 350km dash to the Chunnel was made in good time and I checked in for my train punctually.

As I drove from the check-in to the terminal I was directed by a UK Customs officer into a large, empty warehouse.

For the Chunnel the UK Customs control is on the French side.

Stopping the engine, I was approached by the uniformed Customs Officer who had obviously taken a course in interrogation and was evidently suspicious of my vehicle and the occupant.

Who was I? – prove it – duly showed my
Passport

Who did I work for? – prove it – duly gave my business card

What did the company do? – prove it – duly gave a brochure

* * *

Where had I stayed? – prove it – duly showed the invoices for the two hotels

At this point the Officer became more interested as the second hotel was in a suburb of Amsterdam.

If I have to explain this point then the reader is not old enough to be reading this book.

What was I doing there? – prove it – showed the congress catalogue

I was then asked to get out of the car and open the boot, being asked who owned the vehicle and informed that any contraband would result in confiscation of the vehicle.

As I got out another Officer asked the other if he should get the garage ready. This caused my heart to jump as this was a precursor to dismantling the car, please see the third paragraph of this chapter.

To my relief this suggestion was refused although a very pretty spaniel was produced to accompany the Officer, presumably his pet.

I was asked to open the boot of the car.

The Officer stood back and waited patiently; his pet canine stood by expectantly.

I released the catch and the boot lid sprung up.

Four spongy feet, released from their captivity sprung to attention to stand erect, quivering like a family of jacks in the box.

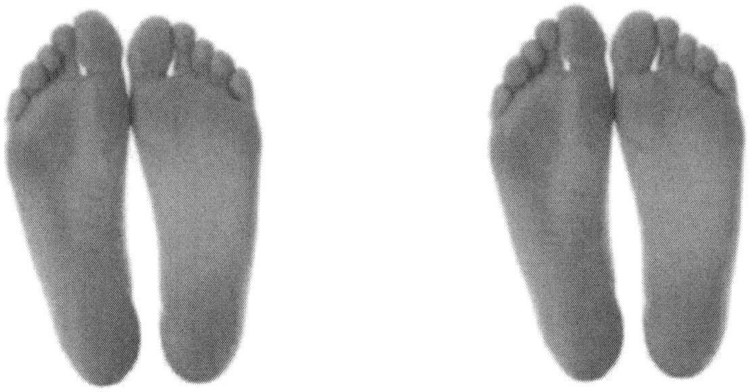

The mutt looked startled at first but was subsequently disinterested, there being nothing to attract his attention.

The Customs Officer, deadpan, asked me 'and what are these Sir?'

Having been taught to answer all questions factually all I could say was 'feet Officer, spongy feet.'

I was sent on my way.

On my return home the vehicle was reassigned to a non-travelling colleague and after a short while was traded in.

I do hope that any new owner did not decide to take the car overseas for a holiday.

CHAPTER 26

A meal to end all meals

We were invited to dinner by our distributor.

The venue was the King David Hotel in Jerusalem.

This hotel is at the top end of the price spectrum having hosted many heads of state and diplomats. The King David Hotel has the reputation as being one of the top hotels in the World.

We were treated to a private dining room and dinner commenced.

Now my colleague and I are fairly hefty chaps with good appetites. The menu was already decided on by our host and was a traditional banquet, so we were not too sure what was to be expected.

The first course arrived. This consisted of a large plate, probably around the size of an old long-playing record, with an indentation approximately 10 centimetres diameter and 5 millimetres deep in the centre which was filled with a cold soup.

We exchanged glances and each grabbed a breadstick from the centre of the table in an attempt to make the effort of scraping the 300 or so microlitres of cold soup into our mouths more profitable.

Having said that the taste of the food was incredible.

Our host had a bemused look on his face.

The first course over, conversation followed whist the attentive waiters removed the plates and some minutes later placed the second course in front of us.

If the first course was on the small side the second course was an attempt to usurp it. A small piece of meat albeit as tasty as the former.

* * *

Once again, the breadbasket received a visit.

The third course matched the second by which time the breadbasket was refilled by the ever-attentive waiters.

At this point I should inform the reader that we had been warned the meal would take around two to three hours.

Before the ninth dish the suspicion dawned on us that this could turn out to be a case of quantity over volume.

The breadbasket was forsaken and by the thirtieth course we were wondering how our stomachs would fit in any further food.

A thoroughly enjoyable meal with good food but one I would like to repeat, without the bread and breadsticks.

CHAPTER 27

Appearances can be deceptive

I would like to leave the Reader with a thought. As the title suggests it pays not to read a book by the cover.

There are many occasions where a little 'front' and the correct dress code will open doors which should be locked shut.

As an example in San Francisco many top hotels have a Manager's Hour in the early evening. By walking into the hotel foyer in a smart suit and wearing a confident demeanour one can partake of the free of charge canapes and drinks unchallenged.

In fact, it is my opinion that one can eat and drink free with a little planning requiring only accommodation for a low cost stay there.

Of course, it can always work the other way.

I should explain that is my habit to always wear a shirt and tie and whenever comfortable a suit when on business. I consider this my uniform and feel more authoritative when wearing it.

A congress in Cairns, a city in Far North Queensland, population around 150,000. Our apartment hotel was directly opposite the Magistrates Court and Police Station.

Being an apartment hotel there were none of the services such as restaurant or bar although the Magistrates Court offered a great breakfast at a reasonable cost providing one was prepared to go through the security check in order to enter the establishment.

The local bar was 100 metres walk away so all creature comforts were readily available.

In addition the Convention Centre was only 200 metres walk in the other direction so all in all a very convenient location.

* * *

The congress was taking place June/July which was the middle of the Australian winter and so the temperature was averaging 20/21 degrees centigrade. This to me was comfortable suit wearing weather.

It was my custom to visit the local bar when the congress finished to partake of a little light refreshment before changing into casual clothing for the evening.

For three evenings I had visited the bar and had a few beers then left. On the fourth and final evening I decided to have a couple more, unwinding from the strenuous time I had, enjoying the glorious weather and friendly locals.

Well one beer led to another and after the first four (Aussie beers are only around half a pint) I felt the need to relieve myself out 'back'.

Standing there minding my own business I became aware of another person in the 'dunny', a rather inebriated local.

He looked at me with a puzzled expression and then the light dawned.

There was no malice in his intentions when he leaned over and said in the laid back drawl only Australians can muster 'Didya gettorf mate?'

Rather than explain the whole situation and being in a somewhat precarious position as I was halfway through the reason for my visit to this particular room I replied in the affirmative.

Hearing this he slapped me on the back in congratulation.

Leaving the little boys room I found that he had also stood me a beer.

It just goes to show you can dress for free drinks.

CHAPTER 28

Sydney's finest

In the previous chapter I mentioned an apartment hotel. These are quite popular in Australia and New Zealand, offering greater freedom and lower cost for accommodation.

As they require a reduced level of staff, check in/out and room servicing, the overheads are lower and this reduction in cost is passed on to the guests.

In many cases the rooms are self-contained apartments, some with laundry facilities and many with kitchenettes.

Personally I enjoy the freedom these hotels offer, particularly when there is a good supermarket in the vicinity giving me the opportunity to have tea and toast the way I like them in the morning.

In the student quarter in Sydney there was an apartment hotel I had become particularly familiar with. Across the road were a few bars and a shopping complex.

The supermarket there supplied everything I needed for breakfast including crumpets which I have a fondness for when well done.

At 0700 in the morning I was sitting at the table in my kitchenette, halfway through a well done, almost burnt black, crumpet with butter and a steaming hot cup of tea when there was an urgent knock at the door.

Now one can always tell the knock of authority as opposed to the knock of others,

This was certainly a knock of authority and one which suggested the opening of the door sooner rather than later would be advisable.

* * *

I made myself decent and opened the door.

Well I unlocked the door. It was actually opened by six firefighters rushing in to attend to the fire which had been indicated by the smoke alarm in my room as a result of the cooking of said crumpets.

Finding no fire, only a bemused Englishman with a half-eaten crumpet in one hand and a cup of tea in the other the firemen did an about turn and trudged out of the room, the senior officer leaving me with a stern warning about the dangers of cooking crumpets.

I finished my breakfast, happy in the knowledge that my room was not on fire and that I was perfectly safe although slightly disturbed by the fact that my fire alarm whilst indicating an inferno to the hotel reception, who saw no necessity to phone me to check if all was ok, made no sound in the room proper.

CHAPTER 29

I tell you, it was that big

I remember an advertisement for a beer a few years ago.

The scene was a bar in Australia where all the customers were crossing their legs to avoid going to the loo.

A stranger appears and asks for the toilet.

He is directed by the bar steward to the dunny out back.

On opening the door he is confronted by a giant hairy spider who waves one of his legs and welcomes him with something like 'hello there!'

Whilst Australia is full of dangerous spiders, (a friend once considerately informed me that there were only two types of creatures in Australia. The dangerous ones and the not-quite-so-dangerous ones), one of the largest and not-quite-so-dangerous is the Huntsman.

In my opinion the arachnid starring in the aforementioned advertisement was a Huntsman.

The Huntsman in Australia can have a leg span of up to 15cm and closely resembles a tarantula in appearance but is not considered a particularly dangerous species as it is not usually aggressive, tending to be more defensive. Bites from Huntsman spiders do not usually require hospital treatment.

Having said that, their appearance is certainly intimidating.

I was in Sydney in the early 2000's.

I was on a business trip and my future wife came along to see what I actually did when I travelled and as a break for her.

* * *

Most days whilst I was out working my partner would entertain herself shopping and visiting the sights, both man-made and natural, which Sydney had to offer.

On this one occasion we travelled together to a business meeting with the local representative.

The meeting over, we returned to the car, my future wife opened the rear door and sat in the back of the car.

I went to the front passenger door and opened it.

The local representative opened the driver's door, let out a cry of 'FUUUUUUU ...' And slammed the door shut, standing a metre away from the car.

Now when a native Australian yells 'FUUUUUUU ...' it is prudent to assume that an element of danger is in existence.

My beloved was still sitting in the back of the car, a look of total bewilderment on her face.

I opened the back door and hauled her by the scruff of the neck out of the vehicle.

At that stage I felt it reasonable to enquire of my business associate as to the reason for his outburst.

He said nothing but gingerly opened the driver's door of the car.

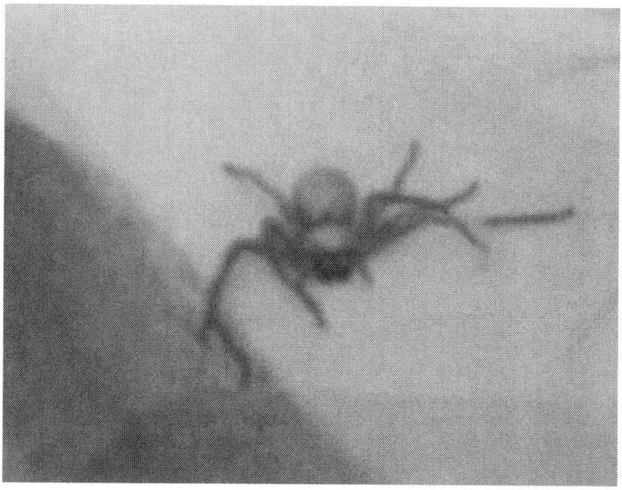

There in the doorjamb sat a huge Huntsman spider.

Perhaps at this stage I should mention that it is my belief that these things can jump.

Two grown men were standing by a car discussing who should try to remove this arachnid from the door.

This discussion continued for some time.

We caught the bus home.

CHAPTER 30

Mind the Door

I will leave you, if I may, with final observations on technological differences.

I find it amazing how certain advances in technology have not been universally adopted, perhaps for cultural or cost reasons.

The one country which epitomizes to me this example is Japan.

I am not referring to high-tech IT based technology, merely everyday designs which have evolved to make life just that little bit more convenient.

A first-time visitor to Japan see many novel designs peculiar to that country which on reflection are logical accoutrements for making life easier whilst taking into account the local culture.

For example, taxi drivers will open the rear passenger door for customers and yet they do not leave the vehicle.

There is a lever operated by the driver which both opens and closes the door and woe betide anyone attempting to close the door manually.

This design, coupled with the immaculate appearance of the driver in cap and white gloves together with napkins on every seat headrest, gives a sombre, respectful aura for all concerned.

Space is at a premium with a large population in relation to the non-mountainous area available for habitation. Therefore it is common to see not only ramps permitting two-tier care parking n the street but also a similar arrangement for bicycles.

Toilets can be interesting. Some fulfil the full range of services including bidet and blow dry whilst others play 'muzac' on locking the door to hide the sounds from within the water closet, preventing embarrassment to the occupant.

One piece of technology which has found its' way here over the past few years offers one of my 'moments'.

Kobe, 1994, the same visit as in Chapter 15.

Yet another congress with a colleague who, in the course of our journey on the Portliner public transport train from the Exhibition Centre to our hotel in Sannomiya, some 5 stops, had managed to mislay his ticket.

Twice a day for the whole week we had religiously inserted our tickets into the slot, walked through and seen no effect this had.

i.e. nothing opened, nothing lit up, nothing happened.

My colleague decided that rather than search his pockets for the ticket he would just walk through.

All hell broke loose, a deafening alarm exploded into life and from nowhere a pair of low steel grips came, one from either side of the barrier, and prevented egress.

I would ask you to picture here the height of these grips.

Due to the physiological height difference between Occidental and Oriental people the grips were far below his chest height yet well above his knees.

I would say that if he had been a split second earlier he would have lost his manhood.

As it was I believe that he was sorely bruised in the nether region.

Miraculously the ticket was found, inserted and exit from the station was permitted with no further drama.

CHAPTER 31

Postscript

27th April 2001

I'm sitting in a coffee bar in Tokyo, after working hours, paradoxically drinking a beer. I am reaching the last leg of a business trip, which has included Dubai, Colombo, Singapore and Tokyo. One more stop, Hong Kong, then home after 3 weeks away, if home is what I can call the United Kingdom anymore.

I am smoking my umpteenth cigarette of the day, Friday I believe. At least I can remember the day of the week! The trip, so far, has been successful and I am at a loss as to what to do this evening: write my notes; complete my expenses; find a really expensive restaurant (not difficult in Tokyo); get drunk (again expensive) or return to my room and try to locate a TV programme in a language I can understand.

After some reflection, and another beer, I think that I'll put my (non) literary talent to some use and write this. How long it will be I really don't know. Perhaps it will peter out and end up as just another wasted part of a tree, to be discarded on my return. Maybe I'll have the time, and inclination, to finish what I've started.

I'm looking at a young Japanese girl at the adjacent table whose ear is glowing alternately blue and red. It transpires that this colourful effect is emanating from the aerial of her mobile phone, something I have never seen before. This reminds me of a conversation I'd had in a bar, somewhere in the World, a few months previously with some associates. I won't name them for two reasons; firstly, they might be embarrassed and secondly,.... I cannot remember their names.

Anyway, I digress. The conversation was on the topic of experiences enjoyed, or not as the case may be, by all travellers, especially those who travel frequently. We all agreed that the frequent traveller takes many experiences as commonplace although they would either fascinate, or be disbelieved by, those who travel less frequently.

* * *

I define those who travel in excess of three months a year, year on year, as frequent travellers and not the regular holidaymaker, who is cosseted from Luton to Malaga, and then back again.

I do not look down on holidaymakers, I have been one myself; I merely consider their travel experiences to be less. At the same time, I appreciate that many of my experiences could be considered naïve to others who have spent a longer time in individual countries I have visited. It is for that reason that I differentiate between travellers and ex-pats.

However, I am writing this and not them.

I can assure you that every incident contained herein is as factual as my memory will permit it to be. Certain identities may have been changed slightly to protect individuals, but the essence is unaltered.

I do not seek to insult or offend any individual, race or religion. I only look to introduce the uninitiated reader to the superficial, and not so superficial, differences and idiosyncrasies one encounters when travelling with what I consider to be humorous and entertaining anecdotes as examples.

If you wish this forms a semi-autobiography although I am not so vain as to believe that anyone outside of my immediate family, and probably not even them, would have any interest in this whatsoever. This narrative is intended to be the biography of all Frequent Travellers (now promoted to capital letters).

I also apologise for any of the views that may be considered by anyone to be sexist, racist, ageist (or any other 'ists' which I have omitted) other than realist, for that is what I consider myself to be.

If all else fails, then I will bequest to my children my account of why I missed a great deal of their formative years.

Printed in Great Britain
by Amazon

68145487R00054